WHY GOOD PEOPLE
CAN'T GET
JOBS

PETER CAPPELLI

WHY GOOD PEOPLE
CAN'T GET
JOBS

The Skills Gap and What Companies
Can Do About It

Wharton
DIGITAL PRESS
Philadelphia

Published by Wharton Digital Press
The Wharton School
University of Pennsylvania
3620 Locust Walk
2000 Steinberg Hall-Dietrich Hall
Philadelphia, PA 19104

Ebook ISBN: 978-1-61363-013-6
Paperback ISBN: 978-1-61363-014-3

To Michael and Bo

Contents

Preface

Many of the important ideas that now dominate the discussion of workplace issues emanated from employer organizations and consulting firms. Often these organizations identify important new trends, and often they make sweeping pronouncements about issues that are thought to be very much still in debate in the academic world. This book grew out of a series of columns I wrote for *Human Resource Executive* magazine in response to various stories in the press about skill shortages. The editors at the *Wall Street Journal* then asked me to write an extended story exploring the evidence for the claim that employers simply could not find candidates with the skills to do the jobs they needed to fill. That article led to a follow-up story, and that, in turn, led my colleague Steve Kobrin to suggest this book. I corresponded with hundreds of people who commented on the *Wall Street Journal* article, and many of their stories appear here.

Thanks to Steve and to Shannon Berning at Wharton Digital Press and to John Wright for their help with this project; to Stacia Edwards and Arne Kalleberg for reading the manuscript; and to Jason Dickhaut for help chasing down the references. Thanks also to the World Economic Forum annual meeting in Davos for hosting a session on this topic.

And here's to the current generation of job seekers, and to the employers who need to hire them. May the two groups work out arrangements that better serve both their interests.

Peter Cappelli
Philadelphia

Introduction

In October 2011, I wrote an article entitled "Why Companies Aren't Getting the Employees They Need" for the *Wall Street Journal*'s annual "Report on Leadership." In it, I noted that even in a time of dangerously high unemployment, companies complain that they can't find skilled workers and sometimes need months of hunting to fill a single mid-level job. I repeated the litany of complaints commonplace in recruiting circles: schools aren't giving kids the right kind of training; the government isn't letting in enough highly skilled immigrants; even when the match is right, prospective employees won't accept jobs at the good wages offered. The list goes on and on. No doubt about it: finding good candidates who will work at a wage that still allows a company to make money is really hard to do.

In my article, I explained the conventional wisdom about what has become known as the "skills gap." I also challenged that notion—because when we look at the facts, there is no evidence to support it. "The real culprits," I wrote, "are the employers themselves. With an abundance of workers to choose from, employers are demanding more of job candidates than ever before. They want prospective workers to be able to fill a role right away, without any training or ramp-up time. To get a job, you have to have that job already. It's a Catch-22 situation for workers—and it's hurting companies and the economy."

My article drew more than 500 responses. Clearly, I had struck a nerve, and not only in readers struggling to get a job themselves. A remarkable number of those who wrote to me were in hiring positions, including recruiters. They reported that their organizations had shortages of employees because the companies had unrealistic standards and would not train or invest in candidates who could otherwise do the jobs. My favorite e-mail came from somebody in a company that had 25,000 applicants for a standard engineering position of whom the staffing people said not one was qualified. Could that really be possible?

Several people—all CEOs—wrote in to say that the problem with hiring is that the American education system is so bad. I have been following this topic since I worked on a US Department of Labor commission in the 1980s. On average, employers who are actually doing the hiring were not then, and are not now, complaining about the lack of academic skills among job applicants. It is mainly other things that they see as important, in particular the lack of work experience. One cannot get work experience in school, and that is where training comes in. Furthermore, almost none of the employers who wrote to me are looking for recent graduates. They want experienced workers.

A few employers reported that qualified candidates will not take the jobs at the wages companies offer them. At this point, it may be necessary to remind these employers how markets work. There is a difference between saying, "We can't find anyone to hire," and saying, "We can't or don't want to pay the wages needed to hire." Just as there is no shortage of diamonds even though they are expensive—you can buy all you want at the market price—not being able or willing to pay the market price for talent does not constitute a shortage.

Virtually all those who wrote to me, especially those close to the hiring process, said something new: that there were serious problems with employer practices. Beyond unrealistic expectations, many also complained about applicant-tracking software and other computerized systems that screen applications electronically. Employers are overwhelmed by applications, and there is no way they can go through them all manually. So they use these systems to help. The downside is that the screening criteria are imperfect. Typically the screening software looks for key words, and if an applicant doesn't include the right key words, out goes his application. One reader who wrote to me described how he had been told he was perfect for a given position—except for the fact that his previous job title didn't match that of the vacancy, which was a title unique to that particular company.

A Failure of Imagination

The workers-jobs disconnect now plaguing the American economy is rich with such anecdotes, many of them ridiculous on their face but debilitating in practice, both to job seekers and to employers. But the disconnect also has a statistical face. In this book, I drill deeper into existing jobs data, probe the problem more broadly, and map a way forward. I use both data and anecdotes—and interviews with jobs professionals—to break through the rhetoric and explore where the true impediments lie.

Is there really a skills gap? To what extent is the hiring process being held hostage by unrealistic hiring expectations, low wages, and automated software that can crunch thousands of applications per second without perhaps truly understanding any of them? What could best bridge the gap between employer expectations and applicant realities, and critically, who should foot the bill for it? In the final chapter, I lay out a series of solutions that can help us break through what has become a crippling employer-employee standoff.

Part of my interest in the subject is professional and academic. As the George W. Taylor Professor of Management at the Wharton School and codirector of the National Center on the Educational Quality of the Workforce during the Bush and Clinton administrations, and through countless commissions, symposia, and studies, I have been tracking the paradoxical forces bearing down on the American workplace: on the one hand, employers who say they can't find the qualified workers they need; on the other, willing and qualified workers who often can't find work for love or money. Even as the economy haltingly recovers, that gap grows wider.

Part of my interest, I should admit, is personal. In my own family, my son couldn't find a real job with his new college degree in classics, so he looked to one of the technical fields in health care that had been identified as hot, where employers (the media assured) were struggling to hire. He went back to school, at a community college, and got a skills certificate in that field—only to discover that it was not hot. Employers were hiring only applicants who already had job experience, and most were interested only in candidates who had certificates in two areas, as the employers were consolidating two occupations into one. Would my son have been better served if he had spent his college years learning to read tarot cards instead of plowing through *The Aeneid*? If we focus only on his employment options, it's a question worth asking.

In the larger sense, though, my interest is societal. When the staffing company ManpowerGroup reports that 52 percent of US employers surveyed say they have difficulty filling positions because of talent shortages, society as a whole has a problem. When the utility industry concludes that 30 to 40 percent of all its employees will be eligible to retire by 2013—and industry experts warn of a subsequent immense gap in knowledge and ability that will be extremely difficult to fill—we all have a problem ready to walk right in the front door.[1] And when millions of unemployed job seekers find it impossible to get the kind of jobs they were performing just a couple of years before and a generation of college graduates, many of whom would have been snapped up by employers in normal times, remain unemployed or vastly underemployed, society has a huge problem as well.

How do we move forward from here? How can we get America's job engine revved up again? It requires a change from business as usual to a fresh way of imagining the employer-worker interface. Blaming schools and applicants isn't the solution, and the way we're doing things now just isn't working. As the old adage goes, the definition of insanity is repeating the same action time and again and expecting different results. The new way will demand more from employers, but it makes good financial sense for them to do it.

CHAPTER 1

Why Aren't the Vacancies Being Filled?

We all know the basics: Four years after the onset of the Great Recession, US businesses are posting record profits even as unemployment remains stubbornly high. In fact, "jobless recoveries" such as we are now undergoing are nothing new. The phrase was coined after the 1991 recession, when it took several years for jobs to come back despite growth in the economy. A similar lag in hiring happened after the 2000/2001 recession. But this time, we're told, is different. It is not that jobs don't exist; what is missing are qualified people to fill them. Drug manufacturer Ben Venue Laboratories, for example, looked to fill 100 openings in Ohio but found only 47 of the 3,600 applicants to be qualified. A large proportion failed the basic reading and math skills test. CEO Thomas J. Murphy noted, "You would think in tough economic times that you would have your pick of people."[2]

An employer survey reports that two-thirds of manufacturers say it is difficult to find qualified job applicants. A study of fast-growing companies says that finding qualified candidates is the companies' biggest impediment to growth. By some calculations, these millions of unfilled jobs are costing the economy billions of dollars in lost business.[3]

Yet for every story about an employer who can't find qualified applicants, there's a counterbalancing tale about an employer with ridiculous hiring requirements. One of my favorites is a job ad for a cotton candy machine operator—if you've never seen cotton candy made, it is not rocket science—where the requirement for applicants was demonstrating prior success operating similar cotton candy machines. To test whether his company's hiring standards were too high, a Philadelphia-area human resources executive applied anonymously for a job in his own company. "I didn't make it through the screening process," he notes.

What's going on? Why can't we make this marriage work? Well, one impediment is the simple math of the situation. Here's how it works: Productivity is typically measured by how much output we get per worker. It always grows coming out of a recession because employers lay off people in the downturn and delay hiring in the upturn, giving those who remain on the job more work to do as business picks up. Productivity growth was nonexistent in the first years of the recession—not surprisingly, as employers were cutting capacity—but rose a healthy 3.5 percent in 2011, in part because business was picking up a bit and employers were getting more work done with fewer people. In all, US productivity was 6.7 percent higher at the beginning of 2012 than it was in 2008, when the Great Recession was in full swing. The way to think about this is that a typical employer can now do almost 7 percent more business without hiring anyone new.

Some of that productivity is due simply to working people harder, and it will be difficult to sustain in the long run, which is why productivity growth tends to slow as the economy grows. But some of it is real and will persist. To the extent that there is any new normal in terms of the need for labor, postrecession productivity is what is behind that need.

Seven percent productivity growth would be an overall good thing, except that the companies don't have 7 percent more business. The US economy as measured by gross domestic product (GDP) was only 1.2 percent bigger at the beginning of 2012 than it was in 2008, but with productivity 6.7 percent higher, employers need 5.5 percent fewer workers now than they did in 2008.

What makes that gap worse is that the population and the workforce keep growing. All that talk in the late 1990s and 2000s about a growing shortfall in the labor force was a myth. The US population grows by about 140,000 new people each month and is about 4 percent bigger now than it was at the end of 2008. In normal times, the labor force would grow at about that same rate.

Putting these facts together yields the following: Employers need roughly 5 percent fewer workers now than at the beginning of the recession, yet there are roughly 4 percent more people who could want jobs. Since the unemployment rate was already about 5 percent when the financial meltdown that led to the recession began, the current unemployment rate should be that baseline 5 percent plus 6.7 percent (from productivity gains) plus another 4 percent (for population growth) minus 1.2 (for the growth in GDP over the four years in question—the only good news in the calculation), for a grand total of 14.5 percent.

Why isn't unemployment that high? Because many people who want jobs have stopped looking and therefore don't count as unemployed. That's also why the unemployment rate, which measures the percentage of jobless actively looking for work, will remain stubbornly high even as the jobs picture improves: some of those who gave up looking will come back into the workforce as new jobs become available, keeping the number of people looking for work high even as more people find jobs.

The more interesting question is what happens where there are jobs to be filled. There are always job openings, even when demand in the economy is falling, because some employees retire, some leave for jobs elsewhere, and some go back to school. Figure 1.1 shows the number of advertisements for job openings, our best guess of real vacancies, versus the number of people who meet the test of being unemployed. These ads are not a perfect proxy for vacancies. Many employers keep job ads posted even when they are not currently hiring, as a way to keep tabs on possible candidates. But this is the best information we have, and it shows what is still a yawning chasm between available work and would-be workers.

Figure 1.1
Labor Supply vs. Labor Demand
US Seasonally Adjusted Data

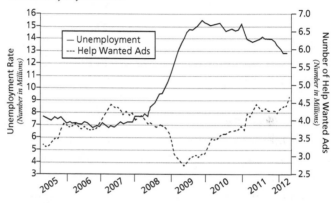

Source: *The Conference Board, BLS. See www.conference-board.org/data/helpwantedonline.cfm.*

The Home Depot Syndrome

Basic math and multicolored charts, though, can go only so far in explaining this chasm. Why? Because this isn't a simple supply-demand issue. When employers have a vacancy to fill, they have many options for filling it. That much should be obvious, but these choices are at the heart of the biggest misunderstanding concerning jobs and hiring.

Many people, especially pundits in the business press, seem to have what we might call a Home Depot view of the hiring process, in which filling a job vacancy is seen as akin to replacing a part in a washing machine. We go down to the store to get that part, and once we find it, we put it in place and get the machine going again. Like a replacement part, job requirements have very precise specifications. Job candidates must fit them perfectly or the job won't be filled and the business can't operate.

This is simply not the way hiring works.

The first and most practical difference between the Home Depot view and the reality of hiring is that unlike the need to replace a part to keep a machine running, jobs don't necessarily have to be filled to keep an organization going. Employers operate with standing vacancies all the time. In some cases, the work gets done by other people, who cover the tasks required by the vacant job. In others, the tasks simply don't get done—new projects get delayed, the expansion of activities is postponed, and so on.

One very real concern about modern business is whether employers even know at which time their failure to fill a vacancy starts to hurt them. Organizations typically have very good data on the costs of their operations—they can tell you to the penny how much each employee costs them—but most have little if any idea of the value each employee contributes to the organization. Revenues and other benefits from operations come in at highly aggregated levels: We know what each profit-and-loss center brings in to the operation, but we have no real idea to which different factors, let alone to each job, we can apportion responsibility for that revenue.

For example, keeping a vacancy unfilled can make an operation appear more profitable because, at least in the short term, costs come down without any decline in revenues or benefits. If we extend this argument, of course, it quickly becomes absurd: Why not lay everyone off? The pressure to fill most vacancies, in fact, does not come from financial arguments, or from math of any kind. It comes from human resource issues—for example, existing employees who are burning out from overwork—or from operating managers pressing to get their new projects under way. Meanwhile, an organizational focus on cost control creates a bias against hiring because we cannot easily track the benefits of filling jobs.

Perhaps the most important difference between the Home Depot model and reality is that unlike a machine part, no perfect fit exists between applicants and job requirements. Put another way, the same tasks can be performed in lots of different ways. In the 1990s, the National Institute of Economic and Social Research, in London, did a series of fascinating studies looking at how companies making almost identical products but operating in different countries got their work done. They found, for example, that US operations used more engineers and more unskilled workers, while German firms used more skilled craftsmen and fewer engineers and unskilled workers to perform the same business tasks. How the companies made the choices that drove those differences is something we'll return to in chapters 4 and 5.

Even when we decide what jobs to fill, job requirements are hardly definitive. We know from studies of employers that when labor is scarce and more expensive, job requirements fall. To prevent bidding wages up, employers are willing to hire applicants with lower skills. When demand is down and applicants are plentiful, job requirements rise as employers expect more from an applicant before they will hire him.[4] During the information technology (IT) job boom of the 1990s, for example, only about 10 percent of the people working in real IT jobs had any kind of IT academic qualifications, no doubt because finding people with such qualifications was difficult and very expensive.

Further, employers almost always have a "make or buy" choice: if they can't find someone with the precise skills they need, they can hire someone with basic abilities and then train her to do the job or, more likely, give him some ramp-up time to learn the job. Employers choose between training versus growing talent based on which is cheaper to do and whether what they want is so unique that it cannot be found in the outside market. If the supply of candidates who have the skills needed to perform jobs grows and their wages fall, hiring candidates with the basic skills and training them afterward loses its appeal.

Bottom line: how employers make such choices plays a big part in determining how long it takes them to fill vacancies.

A Real-World Job Market

The Home Depot view of filling a vacancy might suggest that once you find the right candidate, you hire that person and pay the necessary wage. Supply and demand are equalized through prices, so there should be a clear market wage for each job. Theoretically, there is something to this view. The fact that prices adjust to supply and demand also explains why the notion that there is a "shortage" rarely ever applies in real markets, including the labor market. True, software engineers are expensive, but if you are willing to raise your wages high enough, you can get them.[5]

In the real world, though, employers do not act this way. Candidates, as noted earlier, are not identical, and jobs can be performed in different ways by different individuals with different attributes. Thus, if we shop around sufficiently, we should be able to find someone willing to do the job at a lower wage or someone able to perform the job at a higher standard for the same wage. In more formal terms, we search. We put in the time and effort to find out what the candidates are like, and we wait to make a hiring decision until that information is safely in hand.

Not surprisingly, we spend more effort searching when we think it will pay off and also when it is easier to do so. If only one store in town is selling something we need, we are likely to just go to that store and buy it. If dozens of shops are vying for our trade, we are more likely to shop around. Furthermore, when we do start looking, if we find that there is not much difference in the prices and attributes for the items we want, we stop searching and buy. But if we find lots of variation in prices and in the characteristics of those items, we spend more time searching, because we feel it is more likely we will find a deal.

How does this explain why employers might have delayed filling vacancies following the Great Recession? Because searching has gotten much easier and cheaper for employers, and therefore they search longer, or at least differently. One consequence of so many qualified applicants coming to them is that employers have cut back their own efforts at finding qualified candidates. In Figure 1.2 we can see the decline in the intensity with which employers recruit applicants for a given vacancy:

Figure 1.2
Recruiting Intensity Per Job Vacancy
January 2001 to May 2011

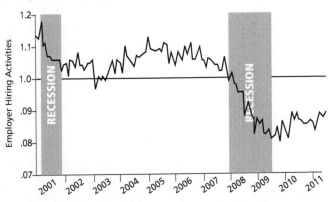

Source: *Steven J. Davis, Jason Faberman, and John Haltiwanger using data from the Job Openings and Labor Turnover Survey. Recessions, as dated by the National Bureau of Economic Research.*

Note: *Data for the Nonfarm US economy excluding the federal government.*

Simply put, employers may take longer to fill vacancies not because no one fits their requirements, but precisely because there are so *many* qualified applicants and because they differ so much. In this case, it might pay off for employers to wait for someone who is perfect for the job, not merely qualified, or even to see who will do the job at a wage well below market rate. This situation is not unlike that of teenagers who think they have many possible dates for the prom, putting off asking anyone in particular while considering their options. Employers, too, can be so dazzled by the choices that they wait too long to fill positions, especially because they cannot easily see the costs of not filling them.

Pundits contend that the existence of vacancies proves that something must be wrong with the possible candidates, or else the jobs would have been filled. They have said this after every recession in recent history, and they are always wrong. It pays to search, especially when the pickings are good.[6]

Competition for Jobs in the Market Is Relative

There's an old joke in business strategy about two men running away from a grizzly bear. One says, "I don't know how much longer I can outrun that bear," and the other says, "Hell, all I need to do is outrun you." The idea is that competition is relative, and that's true in labor markets as well. The fact that candidates differ, that job requirements are fuzzy, and that people with more skills than are required for a job can do it equally well or better than others means that hiring managers can take their time searching for the best candidate.

This relative aspect of the search process is also a big reason why perfectly qualified applicants can't get hired: Why should I hire someone well qualified to do a job when I can hire someone who is overqualified? The experience in the Great Recession in this regard is very similar to what happened in prior periods of high unemployment, especially in the 1970s and '80s, when baby boomer college graduates flooded the labor market and ended up doing jobs that required much less than a college degree.

The fact that competition among job applicants is relative is also behind the well-publicized finding that unemployment rates for college graduates are a fraction of the level for those with only a high school degree or less. The implication some draw from such reports, again using the Home Depot model, is that there must be lots of jobs requiring college degrees relative to the number of people with those degrees. The reality is that the lower unemployment rate for college graduates comes from the fact that college graduates can also do the jobs that require only a high school degree, and arguably do them better, so they win the competition for those openings. When applicants far outnumber job openings, the overqualified bump out those only adequately qualified.

Much of the concern about candidates being over-qualified centers on academic degrees. The percentage of employees who are overqualified for their jobs, as defined by having at least three more years of education than is required by the job they hold, is about three times greater than the proportion of people who are underqualified using the same criterion. And the proportion of overqualified has more than doubled over the past generation.[7]

Some people argue that academic credentials are important to recruiters even when the academic skills themselves are not necessary for the job. Being able to complete a college degree is a useful signal of a person's ability to persevere and complete tasks, even if the skills gathered in college are not relevant to the job in question. Certainly there is evidence for this view. Those who actually get their degree do much, much better in the labor market than those who have many years of college courses under their belt yet don't get the degree. The most compelling evidence that a college degree signals something beyond academic achievement comes when looking at students who get a general equivalency diploma (GED), basically a high school diploma but obtained by taking a standardized test. They do not earn higher wages than those with no GED, and their wages are well below those of traditional high school graduates.[8]

Given all this, it might make sense to get a college degree, even if there are no jobs that require such degrees, because then one can beat out those who do not have degrees. If everyone does this, of course, we have something like an arms race, where individuals and their families invest in credentials that are not required for the jobs they end up doing but that may nevertheless be necessary for them to obtain those jobs. How extensive this situation is stands at the center of a long debate between economists, who see educational investments as largely necessary to meet job requirements, and sociologists, who see these investments as signaling attributes such as persistence.

In a down labor market, the rush to improve credentials heats up in part because the unemployed have both the need and the time to go back to school and get further credentials and in part because employers, with more applicants for their jobs, can be pickier. The level of this competition has reached new heights with efforts to get work experience—arguably the hardest credential to get because it typically requires having done a job already. Thus, the dilemma so familiar to first-time job seekers: How do I get the experience required to get a job in the first place?

Into this gap come unpaid internships, most of which probably violate the Fair Labor Standards Act, which requires that individuals must be paid for work that benefits business employers. These internships are so popular now that an industry has sprung up in which people actually pay for the benefit of finding an unpaid experience so that they will eventually be more desirable to employers.[9] But even here the competition can be ferocious. One college career counselor told me, "The more elite employers expect candidates for internships to have already had an internship somewhere else"—yet another instance of employers being picky and wanting candidates who can make immediate contributions. And remember, many of these are *unpaid* jobs.

The quirkiest consequence of this relative competition for jobs is the growing discrimination against unemployed job applicants, a phenomenon now so prevalent that federal regulations are being considered to address it. Here we see the signaling idea in a different form: Some people who are currently unemployed were let go from their last jobs because they were not good workers, and some may have gotten a bit rusty in their business knowledge. So why should we take a chance looking at unemployed applicants when there are so many other qualified candidates in the queue? Again, perfectly capable people can't get jobs because employers have so many qualified applicants that they can afford to overlook an entire category of applicant.[10] This type of discrimination goes hand in hand with the difficulty that older workers have in getting hired, despite their skills and experience—which are exactly what employers say are in short supply.[11]

Given all this, is it any wonder that a disconnect exists between workers and jobs today? Hardly, but blaming the victim only makes matters worse.

CHAPTER 2

The Skills Gap Debate
Deconstructing Demand

I magine a headline that read, "Happy Employers Deluged with Qualified Applicants." Would the story lead the evening news show? Not a chance. Turn that teaser around, though—"Employers Can't Find Applicants"—and suddenly you have a man-bites-dog story. Upward of 16 million people, most of them until recently gainfully employed, are currently searching for jobs—and *still* employers can't find anyone qualified to work for them. There must be a—*ta-da!*—skills gap. But is there?

Let's start with the headlines themselves. One large reason these stories persist, apart from the fact that they seem so surprising (at least upon a first encounter), is that the journalists involved rarely dig beyond the press releases that spark their interest. Reporters take an employer's word for it that no one who applied could do a given job. We don't know if the employer's expectations were unrealistic, if they failed to look very hard for candidates, or if there was some other simple explanation for their problem, such as their offering too-low wages.

When we look a little more broadly, it looks more like there is evidence of a skills gap. "The Ill-Prepared US Workforce," by the business and research association the Conference Board, reports, for example, that about half of all employers believe that *the people they have hired* are inadequately prepared for their jobs. The Manpower survey cited in the previous chapter concurs. Among the 52 percent of US employers who say they have difficulty filling positions, the most common complaint is "talent shortages." At a minimum, a lot of employers seem to be saying the same thing.

Maybe most telling of all—and most worrisome in the new global economy—is the fact that the skills gap appears to be worse in the United States than in most other countries. As Figure 2.1 shows, the United States ranks seventh among 39 countries measured by frequency of employer complaints about an inability to fill jobs—below Japan, India, and Brazil, but well above such Eurozone powers as Germany, and experiencing more than double the frequency of complaints as registered in the new global rising power, China. The evidence is also puzzling, though, because it is out of sync with the experience of other countries. The rate of complaints in the United States is more than three times greater than in Scandinavian countries, for example, despite the fact that the United States has roughly three times more people searching for each job.

Figure 2.1
Difficulty Filling Jobs by Country

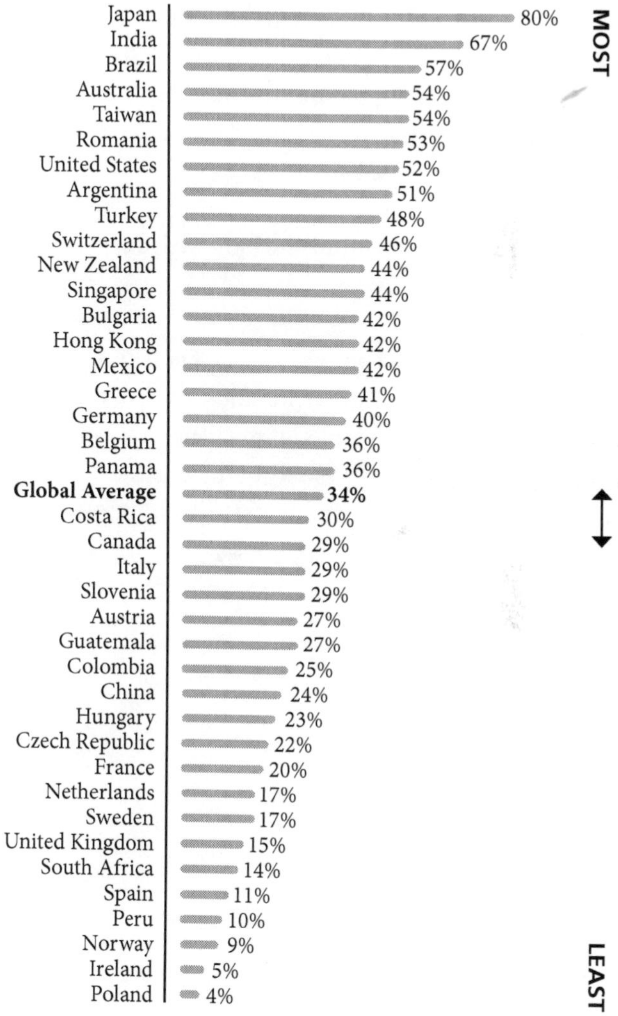

Country	%
Japan	80%
India	67%
Brazil	57%
Australia	54%
Taiwan	54%
Romania	53%
United States	52%
Argentina	51%
Turkey	48%
Switzerland	46%
New Zealand	44%
Singapore	44%
Bulgaria	42%
Hong Kong	42%
Mexico	42%
Greece	41%
Germany	40%
Belgium	36%
Panama	36%
Global Average	**34%**
Costa Rica	30%
Canada	29%
Italy	29%
Slovenia	29%
Austria	27%
Guatemala	27%
Colombia	25%
China	24%
Hungary	23%
Czech Republic	22%
France	20%
Netherlands	17%
Sweden	17%
United Kingdom	15%
South Africa	14%
Spain	11%
Peru	10%
Norway	9%
Ireland	5%
Poland	4%

MOST

LEAST

Source: Manpower 2011 Talent Shortage Survey

The question, though, is this: Do studies like this one show that the United States is among the world leaders in skills gaps or simply in employer whining and easy media acceptance of employer complaints? This brings us deeper into the investigation: to the alleged components of the skills gap itself, at least from the demand side. Let's address the claims one by one.

Myth: Employers can't find workers with adequate skills to fill available jobs.

This assertion is fundamental to the skills gap contention, and yet the more we look at the underlying evidence for it, the more it tends to fall apart. Consider this breakdown, in Table 2.1, also from the massive Manpower survey, of the jobs that are reported to be most difficult to fill.

Table 2.1
Top 10 Hardest-to-Fill Jobs Globally

Position	2006	2010	2011
Technician	3	3	1
Sales Rep	1	2	2
Skilled Trade	5	1	3
Engineer	2	4	4
Laborer	N/A	10	5
Management/Executive	10	8	6
Accounting & Finance Staff	9	5	7
IT Staff	6	—	8
Production Ops	4	6	9
Office Support	7	7	10

Source: Manpower 2011 Talent Shortage Survey

"Laborer," in the "Position" column, is about as unskilled a job category as we can get, while "production operator" is a factory job, typically semiskilled. It is difficult to imagine what the skill gap could be here. A "sales rep" certainly has unique abilities, but these are learned through practice on the job. "Technician" and "skilled trade" are clearly skilled jobs, but here again those skills are learned largely on the job. "Engineer" and "accounting/finance" workers learn their skills at least in large measure in postsecondary classrooms. "Office support" jobs, basically clerical work, might be filled at least in part by hiring high school graduates. Overall, this mix of jobs does not suggest any pattern with respect to skill requirements that would explain the skill shortage complaints.

Myth: Employers can't find workers willing to take jobs at the going wages.

About 11 percent of the employers reporting skill shortages in the Manpower survey said that their problem was that applicants were not willing to accept job offers at the wage the employer wanted to pay. Given what we know about the difficulty all respondents have in recognizing problems that are actually their own fault, the real percentage of employers who have difficulty hiring because they are not offering adequate wages is likely to be much, much higher. When I hear stories about the difficulty in finding applicants, I always ask employers if they have tried raising wages, which in many cases have not gone up in years. The response is virtually always that they believe their wages are high enough.

But—and it's a big *but*—this doesn't reflect a skill shortage. It simply means that employers are not paying the market wage. They may be willing to shop around to see whether someone will take jobs at below-market wages, they may not be able to pay the market wage, or perhaps they just feel they should not have to do so. But their not doing so does not indicate any skills problem with the applicants.

Consider the story in the press of Mechanical Devices, a parts supply company that was unable to fill 40 machinist jobs. That employee deficit was apparently holding back company sales by an estimated 20 percent. The jobs reportedly paid $13 per hour, which might sound good, but the Bureau of Labor Statistics reports that the average wage for such jobs is more than $19 per hour, almost 50 percent higher than Mechanical Devices was offering. Would that have had some effect on the company's ability to find candidates? You bet. A similar, widely circulated story, about the airline Emirates, reported that US job fairs for cabin crew positions, which do not require initial skills, had attracted only about 50 people each. That might sound like evidence that job seekers in the United States just don't want to work. But the jobs required applicants to move to Dubai, which is a significant hurdle for most Americans. Was the pay rate of $2,500 per month enough to have made the move worthwhile? Ask yourself the same question.

In many industries where workers are scarce relative to demand, wages soar but needs also get met. Skilled mining labor is so scarce, for example, that annual earnings for such workers are soaring to six figures and beyond, doubling in the last eight years alone. Hecla Mining Company CEO Phil Baker notes, "If you don't increase salaries for existing employees, then they go somewhere else." In the mining industry, the competition for skilled labor is international, and wages appear to be higher outside the United States.[13]

The moral, at least in part: Skills aren't the issue; a market-determined wage is. If you pay it, they will come.

Myth: Skill shortages are only part of the problem. Employers must also deal with a lack of knowledge and experience.

Logic suggests that a skill shortage means applicants also have some kind of knowledge shortage. You have to know before you can do. Yet only 15 percent of employers in the Manpower survey who reported having a skill shortage said that lack of candidate knowledge was the most important problem they saw in applicants. That category includes academic knowledge but also knowledge of the particular industry or business. The most important employer complaint about candidates in the Manpower study, almost twice as prominent as the knowledge category, is lack of experience—i.e., the tacit knowledge about how to do a job that comes only from having done it before.

To make an obvious point, if job experience is a major requirement for vacancies, then employers are not looking to fill those jobs by hiring entry-level applicants right out of school. Employers want new hires to be able to start contributing, with no further training or start-up time. That's certainly understandable, but the only people who can do that are those who have done virtually the same job before, and that often requires a skill set that, in a rapidly changing world, may be dying out even as it is perfected. The most important reason good individuals can't get jobs where there appears to be a shortage is that employers are defining job requirements in such a way that applicants need to have done the job already, a fact that dramatically narrows the supply of qualified applicants and unintentionally builds atrophy into the very heart of the workplace.

Myth: Even when workers are skilled, knowledgeable, and experienced—and the pay is commensurate with talent—they are often reluctant to go where the good jobs are.

One jobseeker is 43, married, and the father of two grade-school children. Two years ago his employer, a global brand-name high-tech company, sent him from the Bay Area headquarters, where he had worked for more than a decade, to Austin, Texas. Six months ago, just after his family had moved into a newly purchased home, he was ordered back to HQ. He refused and is now unemployed.

To hear employers talk, his reaction is all too common, and is one reason so much talent and experience sits idle while well-matched jobs go begging. But this ignores the fact that employment is a two-way street. For people taking new jobs, the process is not unlike that for the employer. They have to decide whether the new job is worth it, which includes assessing how much trouble it would be to move but also how long the new job will last. In the late 1990s, evidence emerged that a majority of executives were reluctant to relocate in large part because of fear that the new job would not last long and they would then have to hunt for a new job in a community where they did not have contacts.

This reluctance has increased. Recent evidence suggests that only one in four individuals was willing to relocate for a new job in 2011, a figure roughly half of that in the late 1990s.[14]

To recap, then, the hardest-to-fill jobs appear to be those that often require the least skills, employers are frequently unwilling to offer the wages necessary to attract the skill set they seek, knowledge is evanescent and experience frequently as hard to attain as King Arthur's magic sword, and would-be employees are wary of uprooting themselves and their families for increasingly short-term job security. Is this a skills gap or a reality check about the demand side of the jobs equation? I vote for the latter.

Let's look next at supply.

CHAPTER 3

Workforce Facts and Myths
Parsing Supply

If the demand side of the argument for a skills gap can be summed up in an attention-grabbing (though largely erroneous) headline such as "25,000 Applicants, No One Qualified," the media often express the supply side by borrowing the title of a popular series of movies, *Dumb and Dumber.*

The punditry are quick to paint an ugly picture of the people lining up for jobs. They are described as poorly educated and lacking the skills relevant for employment. Students reportedly arrive on the job market without the basic competency needed to succeed. America's public schools don't prepare students for the job market, failing not just them but, by extension, the nation's employers and society as a whole. Even among those who do continue on to college, too few are graduating, while too many of those who do graduate didn't major in the fields where the jobs are. But wait! The future is going to be even worse, as the knowledge economy demands ever more sophisticated skill sets for economic survival.

By now this supply-side argument has been widely accepted as conventional wisdom. There's just one little problem with the whole package of accusations: there's no good evidence for any of it. Again, let's take up the brief against workforce preparedness and examine the claims one by one.

Myth: Students lack the basic competency needed to succeed in the workplace.

A lack of fundamental abilities is the jumping-off point for all the concern directed at those who have recently left school—but it is also the first item contradicted by statistics. When employers have been asked to list the deficiencies they see in both high school graduates and dropouts, the responses have been quite consistent for decades. Their list is topped not by a cluster of missing technical or academic abilities but by a lack of work attitudes and self-management skills such as punctuality, time management, motivation, and a strong work ethic. Indeed, the absence of these traits, which used to be called "character issues," repeatedly shows up as a primary concern in numerous studies.

Among the most rigorous of the studies looking at employee deficiencies was a 1994 census survey of employers in which concerns about workplace attitudes led the list, while issues related to a lack of academic preparation were far below.[15] Fifteen years later, in 2009, the Business Roundtable conducted a survey asking employers to rank the most important work skills missing among recent high school graduates. Here again, the biggest complaints were about attitudes and self-management skills. We have to go down to the eighth item on the list to find something that might be taught explicitly in schools (oral communication) and 14th on the list to find a traditional academic subject (reading skills). A 2011 study of 540 hiring managers conducted by Harris Interactive for the DeVry Career Advisory Board echoed these findings: Out of the 15 attributes the managers viewed as important for success in their organizations, only one, communication skills, was related to an academic subject.[16]

Certainly fundamental skills such as taking direction and being conscientious about your work are important, but they can also be learned in innumerable situations outside school, including at home. Meanwhile, very little, if any, evidence exists to suggest that basic academic abilities such as communication skills are the cause of hiring problems.[17]

The consistent appearance of the same employer criticisms over nearly two decades suggests that today's workforce is no more fundamentally flawed than the workforce available 20 years ago. It is also entirely possible that these complaints are generally symptomatic of older employers assessing younger applicants. But however you choose to interpret these numbers, it's very hard to walk away with the sense that today's job seekers are critically and uniquely unemployable.

Figure 3.1
Gap Between Importance of Skill and Workers'
Current Skill Level *(as Perceived by Employers)*

Severe Deficit	Personal accountability for work	-29.0
	Self-motivation	-28.0
	Strong work ethic	-28.0
	Punctuality/showing up to work on time	-24.0
	Time-management skills	-24.0
	Professionalism	-23.0
	Adaptability	-20.0
Moderate Deficit	Oral communication skills	-17.0
	Creative problem-solving	-17.0
	Teamwork	-16.0
	Cortical thinking	-16.0
	Job-specific professional skills	-15.0
	Customer/client relationship management skills	-12.0
	Quantitative reasoning	-11.0
Small Deficit	Reading skills	-9.0
	English skills	-8.0
	Job-specific technical skills	-7.0
	Job-specific knowledge	-4.0
	Writing skills	-4.0
	Basic computer skills	-3.0
No Deficit	Specialized IT user skills	0.20
	Management skills	0.30
	Administrative skills	0.30
	Mechanical/machine operating skills	0.90

Source: The Springboard Project, "Lifelong Learning: An Essential Factor in Workforce Success and Global Competitiveness," businessroundtable.org/studies-and-reports/american-worker-survey-telebriefing.

Myth: Public schools are failing their students, their families, the nation's employers, and society as a whole.

Even if most employers are not actually complaining about shortfalls in academic skills, it is still possible that there are problems with graduates. What's more, frequent media reports about the wretched state of American public education make it very easy to generalize that the graduates of these schools arrive on the job market set up for failure. This supposed inadequacy of the nation's schools is also a powerful narrative that plays nicely into the "good old days" bias that says that previous generations were held to higher scholastic standards. But is it true?

Student performance turns on so many factors that it is quite difficult to use any single measure to sum up how students are doing. For example, the success that fourth graders have in math may say nothing about how eighth graders are doing in reading. As a country, we are also pretty unique in leaving education to state and local governments. The federal government provides only about 8 percent of K–12 education budgets, and states each go their own way in setting standards and measuring how their students are doing. Nationwide assessments happen only every few years because they are so difficult to administer.

Still, statistical evidence does suggest that US student performance has actually improved over the past several decades, especially when measured against the dismal performance results during the 1970s. (The 1970s, recall, provided the basis for the famous "A Nation at Risk" report about failing schools.) Ironically, many of the people complaining today about how bad schools are compared to when they were kids—that's anyone in his 50s—were in school when postsecondary education was probably at its worst. In recent years, students' test scores have markedly improved. The best countrywide measure is the National

Assessment of Educational Progress (NAEP), which shows that, for 9-year-olds, proficiency in reading was higher in 2008 than in any year since data were available, going back to 1971. For 13-year-olds, scores have been increasing in recent years, although there have been periods since 1971 when scores were as high. In math, scores for 9- and 13-year-olds were higher in 2008 than in any prior year. The proportion of students taking advanced courses in science and math doubled from 1982 to 2004.[18] Dropout rates tell an even better story, falling by half for low-income students from 1972 to 2009.[19] All these positive trends not only buck the notion that our schools are failing; they also signify that today's employees should arrive on the job market with more of the necessary academic abilities.

Figure 3.2
Dropout Rates
Dropout rates of 15- through 24-year-olds who dropped out of the grades 10–12, by family income: October 1972 through October 2008.

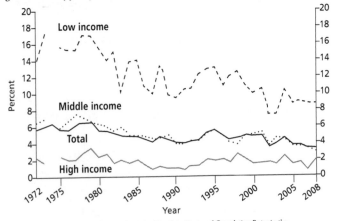

Source: National Center for Education Statistics, Trends in Drop and Completion Rates in the United States, 1972–2008.

But concern over our schools is also driven by the specter of foreign competition and international comparisons that show average US student performance faltering on the global stage. The most accurate of these studies, done by the Organisation for Economic Co-operation and Development (OECD), show US students about in the middle of industrial economies. It is true that we used to be higher up, but our relative fall is largely representative of other countries catching up, especially those in Asia, where, until recent decades, economies and levels of public spending were modest. Meanwhile, there is no evidence of any absolute decline in US scores or even of a sharp decline relative to other countries.

While comparing US average student performance internationally doesn't point to a critical failure in our schooling, it does bring up a large discrepancy in the numbers used to create that ranking. The "US average" is made up of test scores from inner cities and poor states that would be at the absolute bottom of the OECD rankings and of test results from affluent states and suburbs that would be at the absolute top of any ranking. (In fact, the top performers in the international rankings are actually large cities, Hong Kong and Shanghai, and small countries, Singapore and Finland. Korea is the only reasonably large country among the top five academic performers. The United States ranks 16th.[20]) The academic performance of the very best public high school in the city of Philadelphia, for example, is roughly twice as great as the very worst. If we want to improve the scores of the average American student, and future employee, the easiest way to do so would be to pull up the bottom.

Myth: Not enough Americans are graduating from college.

Supposedly inferior elementary and secondary education is only the beginning of the complaints. Employers also criticize the American workforce for being short on college graduates.[21] While the United States sends more high school graduates to four-year colleges than does any other country (about 70 percent), only 57 percent of those graduate six years later. Today about 42 percent of 25- to 34-year-olds have at least an associate college degree. While that may seem to be a large number, it doesn't represent any improvement over their parents' generation. Many developing nations have substantially grown the percentage of their populations with a postsecondary education, another case of the United States appearing to stand still while the rest of the world catches up. Several decades ago, the United States did lead the world in the percentage of individuals with college degrees, but it has now been surpassed by some countries, including Korea, where almost 58 percent of the 25–34 age group has at least an associate degree. (Russia has the highest percentage across all ages combined, which reminds us that an economy's success is not related to education in any simple fashion.) Although it may not signal a catastrophic decline, the low US college completion rate is indisputably

Figure 3.3
Percentage of 25- to 34-Year-Olds with an Associate Degree or Higher, 2008

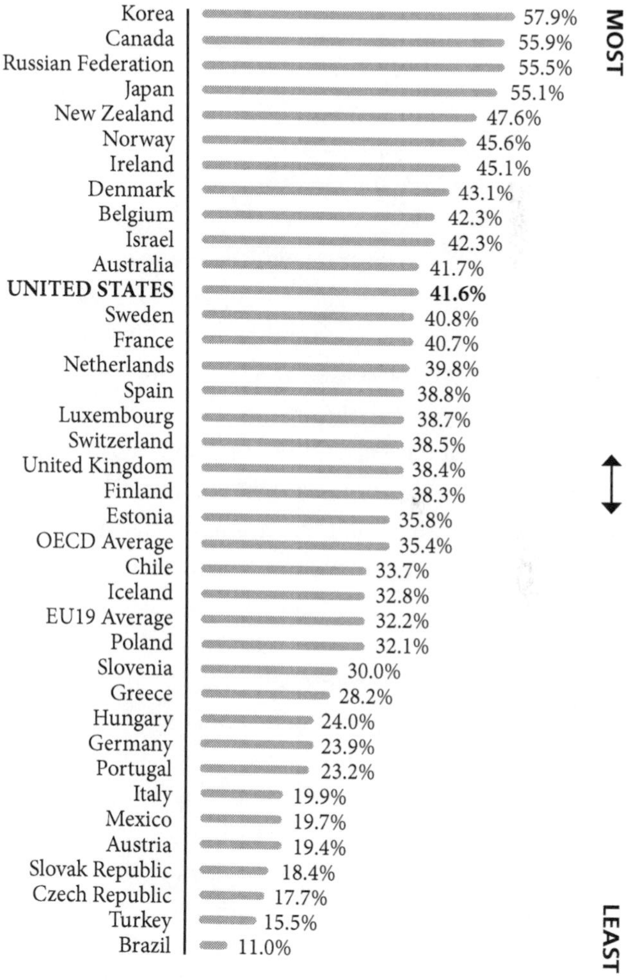

Country	Percentage
Korea	57.9%
Canada	55.9%
Russian Federation	55.5%
Japan	55.1%
New Zealand	47.6%
Norway	45.6%
Ireland	45.1%
Denmark	43.1%
Belgium	42.3%
Israel	42.3%
Australia	41.7%
UNITED STATES	41.6%
Sweden	40.8%
France	40.7%
Netherlands	39.8%
Spain	38.8%
Luxembourg	38.7%
Switzerland	38.5%
United Kingdom	38.4%
Finland	38.3%
Estonia	35.8%
OECD Average	35.4%
Chile	33.7%
Iceland	32.8%
EU19 Average	32.2%
Poland	32.1%
Slovenia	30.0%
Greece	28.2%
Hungary	24.0%
Germany	23.9%
Portugal	23.2%
Italy	19.9%
Mexico	19.7%
Austria	19.4%
Slovak Republic	18.4%
Czech Republic	17.7%
Turkey	15.5%
Brazil	11.0%

MOST — LEAST

Source: Organisation for Economic Co-operation and Development, 2010.

a huge waste of resources. If everyone who started college actually finished, America would be far and away the world leader in college degrees. But whether the economy really needs more college graduates is a different and more difficult question. That we consider next.

Myth: Even among college graduates, too many didn't major in fields where the jobs are.

So what about those employees who made it past high school, persevered through college, and still can't find a job? The easy answer is that they just didn't study the right material, but looking at the trends in what majors students select—or simply asking anyone close to the college world—shows exactly the opposite. For example, business is now by far the most popular college major, and the number of business degrees granted has tripled since 1970. (An impressive growth even when you consider that the number of all degrees doubled in the same period.) There are also 15 times the number of computer and IT degrees awarded, while health-related degrees have quintupled. It is hard to see those changes and not believe that students are responding to the labor market.

On a more granular level, certain seemingly critical subjects have experienced little to no growth. The percentage of degrees in the physical sciences, for example, was flat over that period, while engineering degrees were up only 50 percent. Degrees in both fields have declined as a proportion of all degrees.[22]

Students' apparent lack of interest in these fields is pointed to as cause for concern, but these are hardly new arguments. In the last few decades, many reports have predicted economic damage as a result of a national shortage of scientists and mathematicians, dire warnings that have since turned out to be false. It is certainly true that academic research in science and math abroad is catching up to that in the United States, but this is completely different from suggesting that there is unfilled demand for such science jobs.[23]

In fact, for all the hand wringing, the supposed importance of these jobs has not been reflected in the labor market. A recent review of the evidence finds no basis for concluding that there is anything like a shortfall of such science-minded graduates.[24] Indeed, one highly skilled engineer told me of being advised by his career counselor to remove reference to his PhD from his résumé because his assumed wage demands might scare off prospective employers. The expansion of postdoctoral jobs in universities over the past few years was driven in large measure by a lack of jobs for such graduates. And these students were more often supported in school by government funding than business offers. Veering away from these hard science jobs seems to have been a rational move by workers looking to be employed.

Information technology is another field where complaints about shortages have been common. The IT field has always been volatile, rising and falling not only with the economy but with changing demand for new technologies. What's more, the turnaround time for new graduates (four years) is a lifetime in IT years, often leaving supply out of sync with demand. After the 1991 recession, for example, engineering students noticed the sharp decline in IT jobs, and switched to other majors. That smaller cohort of IT majors graduated four years later, just when the dot-com boom began, driving salaries for IT workers sky-high. On campus, students switched into IT programs in droves, then graduated around 2001, just as the IT market was collapsing. The next generation of students chose other majors, graduating to a chorus of complaints about a shortage of IT skills. What's the lesson taught by this IT employment roller coaster? To assume that there will be the right number of graduates coming out of college with the right skills when you want them and at the wage you want to pay is folly.

A former student of mine, fortunately employed and running a Silicon Valley company, described his company's problem finding applicants with the relevant IT engineering skills. Silicon Valley pretty much invented the "free agent" model of hiring for new skills rather than training and then letting workers go once those skills aren't needed. My ex-student reported sharply rising salaries for software engineers with hot skills in mobile devices and data mining, both areas without enough qualified applicants. But because Silicon Valley's innovation cycle is so fast, it creates a kind of turbocharged version of the complaints heard from other industries about skills not meeting open positions. The question remains the same: Is a slow-reacting workforce to blame for this shortage?

Consider this analogy, drawn from outside the high-tech industry: A car manufacturer decides to buy a key engine component rather than make it. Despite the fact that the component's requirements change every year and the car won't run without it, the company simply assumes the market will deliver the new component on time, matching exact specifications, and at the necessary price. This behavior seems crazy—or at the very least represents a complete failure to manage risk—and yet that's precisely what IT companies have been doing.

Silicon Valley is an industry that demands a very precise, rapidly changing type of employee. Thus Silicon Valley companies ought to keep the schools that provide appropriate graduates informed about what sort of employees they want. They should be involved in co-op programs and support students pursuing the needed courses, and they should train and develop current employees for skills that are emerging. These efforts pay off by ensuring that a regular stream of acceptable employees is available as the industry continues to morph and grow. To expect schools and students to guess what skills your company will need in the future is plain and simply bad business, especially in such a rapidly transforming and innovative industry. In effect, doing so amounts to out-sourcing the supply of talent without bothering to let the outsource vendors know.

Myth: As we enter a knowledge economy that will demand ever more sophisticated skill sets for survival, things will only get worse.

Even if we discount what employers are saying about their current needs, it is possible that future needs might reveal big skill gaps in terms of the preparedness of graduates for the workplace.

I recently participated in a National Academy of Science workshop on the future of skill requirements. A common view imagines the US economy as a giant kitchen where we are following standard recipes to bake a huge number of cookies. Each recipe outlines the proportion of inputs into the production process, including a mix of employees with requisite skills. To increase the production of cookies, we simply add proportionately more of the appropriate skills. Likewise, to figure out what kind of employees we need in the future, we just extrapolate from the expected growth in the economy.

Of course, imagining the economy of the future—and thus the necessary workforce—is far more complicated than linearly expanding a cookie production line. Demand is not just constantly changing; it's almost impossible to predict, especially on a micro level. And while there has been a broad, long-term shift from manufacturing to service jobs, even that trend has been somewhat unpredictably accelerated in the United States by the rise of China. Suddenly, we've found that a lot of our cookies are being made on the other side of the Pacific!

But the surprises don't end there. As manufacturing jobs were moving to China, higher-skilled jobs long considered to be critical to the economy of the future, such as computer programming, have been even easier to offshore to places such as India. To be sure, some very-high-skill and often high-paying service jobs, such as consulting and legal services, have continued to flourish. But other service industries showing real growth (for example, elder care) require very-low-skill workers. As a result, concern mounts that the middle of the labor market has been hollowing out, reflected by the sharp increase in income inequality, and that it will continue. But, even here, we can't be certain, because of the unpredictable nature of changing consumer preferences and foreign competition.

Some trends we can trace, such as a modest overall rise in average employee skill requirements, in part because of the decline in semiskilled manufacturing assembly jobs. There is also some evidence that a move to teamwork and greater employee involvement in many organizations has increased skills requirements, a trend that is also particularly prevalent in manufacturing. But these overall shifts are relatively small, and the talents they point to as important for the future are mainly interpersonal and communication abilities, not the kind of math- and science-based academic skills typically taught in school.

Likewise, the evidence suggests that perhaps 10 to 15 percent of the individuals caught by the rise in the unemployment rate during the Great Recession have a significant mismatch between their previous jobs and where new vacancies lie. But even in that modest gap there can be a possible fit between those workers and newly available jobs. For example, a secretary in a declining manufacturing sector could work in roughly the same capacity in the expanding health-care sector.

Another transformational element, productivity growth, also rattles the straightforward cookie kitchen view of the economy and provides some additional fodder for those screaming loudest about a skills gap. It is true that today we need far fewer workers to turn out the same number of cookies. This means that even in fields that haven't been decimated by offshoring, machines and software can often be substituted for more expensive workers. But understanding this broad dynamic is only so much help in guiding the employees of the future. The answer from a whole generation of studies is quite clear: there is no inevitable direction. The direction depends largely on the choices made by individual employers. Within the same industries right now, some employers choose recipes that require high skills from most employees while others choose ones that require lower-level skills, substituting expert guidance for the skill of the typical employee.

Ultimately, predictions about what skills will be required in the future are based on best guesses, a method that has not been very accurate in the past. At the moment such predictions suggest that service work will continue to grow, some of it high skilled, some of it low skilled, while manufacturing will continue to shrink. Even within the same industries, individual employers are making a range of hiring decisions, with some choosing independent, highly skilled workers while others choose employees with lower-level skills, substituting expert guidance for the skill of the typical worker. With such a mixed message on the abilities and skill levels employees of the future will need, why is the belief that jobs will require much more skill so popular?

Perhaps it easier to see the cases where skills have risen than those generally lower-profile, less-skilled jobs. Perhaps we're also confusing the presence of sophisticated new technology with the skill requirements for the jobs that use it. This new technology may actually *reduce* the necessary skills. Consider word processing, a fancy combination of software and computer technology, which now fixes typos and spelling errors, handles breaks in lines, and formats all automatically, tasks that used to require some real skill from copy editors and typists but can now be done by virtually anyone.

Finally, there is the simple fact that every generation believes it has experienced profound technological changes, perhaps because it was not around to witness the truly unprecedented changes of previous generations. Imagine witnessing the rise of widely available electricity, telephones, and automobiles—all in the same decade. We are constantly reminded that we live during the computer-driven Information Revolution, but there is no evidence that the current period represents one of unusual changes in technology. Likewise, no data or statistics convincingly support the claim that our job seekers are remarkably unprepared for the future, whatever it may be.

However, a boatload of anecdotal evidence suggests that while the workforce is largely competent and able, the hiring process by which supply and demand are brought together is an absolute mess. We go there next.

CHAPTER 4

Something Is Wrong with the Hiring Process

Why can't good people get hired? As we've just seen, the problem does not appear to lie entirely with the individual. There still is a big oversupply of candidates, employers can afford to be picky, and applicants need to be overqualified to have a shot at getting a scarce job. To the extent that employers have concerns about the skills of applicants, they focus on the skills associated with work experience. Lots of reasons argue for improving education, but on balance, employers are not complaining about the academic preparation of applicants. What's more, students appear to be going where the jobs *are* in terms of educational choices. Nor does the problem seem to lie solely on the demand side. Jobs exist, even in this recovering economy, and some of them, employers say, go begging.

If not specifically with supply or demand, then where does the problem lie? Well, one large impediment is the point of connection between the two sides of the jobs equation: the hiring process itself.

As most anyone who has recently applied for a job knows, hiring has changed dramatically in recent years. The Internet has replaced job advertisements in newspapers, one of the key factors driving the financial decline of the latter, and software has replaced most recruiters. Because job applications are done online, applicants rarely talk to anyone, even by e-mail, during the hiring process.

One upside of this automation is that applying for jobs has been made considerably easier, an outcome that was intended in the 1990s, when these systems were born and employers were competing to attract applicants. But there has been an unintended downside: that ease, combined with the huge pool of job seekers, now means that employers are overwhelmed with job applications. At the same time, human resources (HR) departments have been pushed to cut costs, especially their own head count. The only way to meet those two demands has been to move even further toward automating the entire hiring process.

Elaine Orler of Talent Function helps companies build these automated systems, and she describes how they work. First, hiring managers write up descriptions of the job they need to fill. Since hiring managers frequently cannot agree on exactly what they want, the description ends up being vague, a practice that inevitably encourages still more people to apply for the position. Of course, good job descriptions should have "qualifying requirements" that have to be met before an application can even go forward— the requirement, for example, that an applicant have a particular certificate associated with skills training—but, some argue, federal antidiscrimination regulations often pull in the opposite direction. Because such qualifying requirements may be disproportionately associated with protected groups in the population, some employers are afraid to take the risk of imposing requirements that might be sensible but appear to discriminate. So they let virtually everyone apply, and the system becomes clogged with its own largess of applications.

At the same time they are encouraging a tsunami of applications, hiring managers also find it hard to resist including in job descriptions the experiences and skills that will ensure a successful candidate can step right into the job and do everything needed. Especially with the abundance of talent looking for jobs, why not? Here again, though, an understandable impulse pulls in an unintended direction. Neal Grunstra, the founder and president of Mindbank Consulting Group, a staffing and IT projects company, calls it "looking for a unicorn." Managers pile all the credentials and expertise into the job description to minimize the risk that the candidate will fail, making it virtually impossible to find anyone who fits.

Job seeker Kim Hogan has been there. She told me about "one post that has gone unfilled for nearly a year, asking the candidate to not only be the human resources expert but the marketing, publishing, project manager, accounting and finance expert. When I asked the employer if it was difficult to fill the position, the response was yes but we want the 'right fit.'" David Altig, research director at the Federal Reserve Bank of Atlanta, notes that this broadening of skill requirements is now commonplace. Where in the past a company may have had three positions and only one required computer skills, now "one person is doing all three of those jobs—and every job you fill has to have computer skills."[26]

Sometimes the additional requirements seem downright trivial. Fernando Boero, a mechanical engineer with a master's degree, a professional license, and 30 years of experience, describes his recent experience job hunting: "I found a listing for a mechanical engineer with a minimum of three years' experience along with experience with various analysis and design software packages and, more importantly, 65 words per minute typing skills ... When did an engineer need to type so fast to perform his duties?"

The cutbacks in most HR departments now mean that there is rarely anyone left to push back on the hiring manager's job requisition and say, "Are all these skills requirements deal breakers?" In some organizations, the HR department is further disincentivized to push back because it gets held responsible if a new hire fails. In such circumstances, it's often safer to leave the job vacant.

Software-Driven Hiring

Once job requirements have been settled on, however haphazardly, they are then built into the hiring software that screens applications. Some requirements, such as possessing credentials, are easy to write into software, but others, such as the ability to get along with customers, are not, and may require many questions even to get close to an accurate response. And even then, the software might be identifying the wrong qualities actually needed for the vacant position. Tom Keebler at the HR consulting firm Towers Watson, who advises employers about hiring systems, says even well-intentioned hiring managers have a problem trying to identify skills that are not easily associated with credentials or experience.

Once it's in the software, each requirement, critical or trivial, essentially becomes something like a hurdle that applicants have to clear to become a qualified candidate. One job seeker who wished not to be identified described this experience with an employer: "I asked if anyone had done the job yet successfully with the additional duties and they said, 'Yes, the lady who is temping in that position is currently doing all of those duties and she does them well.' So I asked why they didn't hire her and they told me that she failed the online questionnaire (which was mostly about personality fit) so they wouldn't hire her." Apparently doing the job well wasn't enough of a qualification. This was, it should be noted, no isolated tale. Thirty-eight percent of employees in the Business Roundtable survey cited in chapter 3 report that their current employer looks *only* at education and prior experience, rather than directly at skills and abilities, to determine who can do which job.

The criterion placed in these software programs is having actually done the tasks before, not just being able to do them, but woe to the applicant, however able, whose experience and credentials don't form a perfect match with what the software is looking for. Jeffrey Oleander (his *nom de Net*) says, "I once designed and developed a set of tools for software quality testing management but was turned down for [a job] that used a particular brand-name version of just such a tool." Having built such systems wasn't enough, either. Says Oleander, "Another time, I was turned down because I didn't have two years of experience using an extremely simple database report formatting tool, the sort of thing that would require just a couple hours for any half-decent database wrangler to master, less than an hour for the very best."

Another anonymous job seeker described a similar fate: "I was just denied a placement with a company because although I had what it takes according to the human resource [manager] who handled my file, I didn't have the exact same title on my résumé. This specific title is something only that company uses. They are [still] looking to fill this position." But what else, really, is a software program to do? It can't lean back in a chair opposite the job seeker and iron out these little misunderstandings over a cup of coffee.

Then there is the wage issue. Most of these automated systems ask the applicant about the wage he or she thinks is acceptable. Some systems tell the applicants the wage and ask if that is okay. If respondents say no, their application is put aside. Maybe that is reasonable if the employer can't pay more, but labeling such a candidate as unqualified tortures the meaning of "applicant shortage."

In effect, leaving wage questions up to anonymous software creates an auction approach where potential applicants feel as though they are bidding for the job. It's like the old limbo dance challenge: How low can you go? Applicants might win jobs by underbidding the competition, but they are apt to saddle themselves with a wage well below the market rate. Yet if they guess too high, they can be assured that the software will kick their applications out of the running. Damned if they do, damned if they don't.

Beat the Software

How sophisticated are the algorithms used to parse job applications for the right attributes? Mightily so, but they are capricious, too. This Beat-the-Software advice, culled from various experts, should serve as a warning shot across the bow of employers and would-be employers equally.[27] Does anyone benefit from a hiring process that turns on such small distinctions?

- *Don't use headers or footers.* They jam most parsing algorithms.
- *Customize each résumé based on language used in the job description.* If the description says "CPA," make sure "CPA" is on your résumé. Don't go too far, though: copying and pasting the job description won't land you the gig.
- *Use conventional formats.* While fancy fonts, strange layouts, and functional formatting might impress an

employer, computers hate them. Stick to a simplistic style and reverse chronological formatting.

- *Put it in context.* Modern résumé parsers check the context of buzzwords such as Java or C++, so if you want to seem different from the kid who took one "Java" class in high school, go more in depth about what you know and how long you've known it.
- *Submit your résumé in text format.* While .pdf might be convenient, MS Word generally ensures the least parsing errors.
- *Never use graphics.* Graphics always hamper the parsing process and generally show up as white noise to the algorithm. White noise is just what you *don't* want.
- *Include your postal address.* Your address is often how your résumé is filed. If you don't include it, you might not get considered at all.

Hiring by the Numbers

What happens when we string together so many hurdles in the hiring process? For simplicity, let's say that the probability that a typical applicant can meet each of the requirements is 50 percent. The probability that he or she will clear two hurdles is then 0.5 times 0.5 (because they have to clear both) or 0.25. At 10 hurdles, only 1 in a 1,000 applicants will get through, and a typical application has dozens of questions, each one of which is necessary for someone to be considered fully qualified. Remember the company that had 25,000 applicants for a reasonably standard engineering position and staffing people who said none of them was qualified? Could that really be possible? You bet. All one needs for that to happen are 14 requirements in the model just discussed, many fewer if some hurdles are highly specific.

What happens when hiring managers find that no candidate makes it through to the end of the recruiting software screens? Do the managers go back in and pick out those who *almost* made the grade so that they can take a more careful look at them? Elaine Orler points out that doing so can raise legal questions. Employers have to be careful that their recruiting and selection processes do not have an adverse impact on the workforce by disproportionately screening out women, minorities, and other protected groups. One way employers ensure that all applicants are treated fairly is to ensure that all of them are treated consistently. By definition, pulling out selected applicants who have been rejected by the hiring software and reevaluating them means that not all applicants have been dealt with equally—another instance, perhaps, of the perfect being the enemy of the good, or at least the practical.

Is this just a matter of employers being, one, picky in a soft labor market and, two, moonstruck with cost-saving, application-crunching, HR-shrinking technology? In part, yes, except that by doing so, employers are often unable to fill needed jobs, and suffer the costs of not doing so—and there is a hideous waste of talent and experience that comes when able applicants are tossed aside by capricious algorithms. So blame the hiring process, yes, but look deeper. The software might be inevitably flawed, but if employers did more to generate their own solutions, software would not be king. We turn there next.

CHAPTER 5

A Training Gap, Not a Skills Gap

Despite all the concern about the supposed inadequate skill level of job seekers, surprisingly little attention has been paid to the sagging investment in employee training among those companies apparently desperate for skills. "The last company that sponsored technical training that I received was back in 2003," recalls Jim Schmidt, a longtime IT professional, adding, "I can't remember the last time that I even heard of someone taking technical training."

Large-scale, consistent, and credible evidence on employer-provided training is remarkably hard to come by, so it's difficult to know exactly how common Schmidt's experience is, but the data we do have suggests a distinct decline in employer investment in workers. In 1979, young workers received on average about 2.5 weeks of training per year. By 1991, census data found that only 17 percent of employees reporting had received any formal training over the past year. Several employer surveys around 1995 indicate that somewhere between 42 and 90 percent of companies offered some training—the lower number indicating more programmatic training—but the total amount of training an individual received per year averaged just under 11 hours. Additionally, much of this learning was not job specific, instead covering issues such as workplace safety (the most common training topic[28]) and the operational information that vendors provide when they bring in new equipment (as in "Here's how to work this new copier").

Most recently, in 2011, the global management consulting firm Accenture surveyed US employees and found that only 21 percent had received any employer-provided formal training in the past five years. In other words, nearly 80 percent of today's workforce is doing jobs with no recent instruction, if any at all, in five years. There's no reason to think there was much training in the years before that, either.

Particularly hard-hit have been the work-based training programs, such as apprenticeships, that help new employees get up to speed with the demands of a specific job. Mike Collins, a manufacturing expert, recalls that a generation ago virtually all major manufacturers had large-scale apprentice programs. He calculates that even though about 12 million manufacturing jobs still exist in the United States, there are only 18,000 apprentices in manufacturing—the equivalent of just over one-tenth of 1 percent of that workforce.[29]

At the same time that apprenticeships are disappearing, the automation of many manufacturing processes, especially the use of computer-driven machining, has led to increases in skills requirements in those jobs. In many cases, manufacturing now requires additional IT skills to what had previously been hands-on machining jobs. Collins explains: "The problem is that as the lines became more complex, the need for workers with the advanced skills to operate and maintain them also increased. But my experience as a supplier to these large companies is that investment in the training of the new workers has gone down over the last 25 years. In fact, one could say that the investment in training is inversely proportional to the investment in automation. From a machine manufacturer's point of view, this trend has resulted in less preventative maintenance, more emergency breakdowns, and lower-skilled workers."[30] In short, a huge part of the so-called skills gap actually springs from the weak employer efforts to promote internal training for either current employees or future hires.

The Skills Standoff

Some employers continue to provide a great deal of training, but the evidence suggests that, on average, most employers do not, largely to save money. When asked in a Business Roundtable survey why they did not train, employers responded overwhelmingly (76 percent) that costs were the reason. Furthermore, nearly a fifth of those employers indicated that they didn't want to risk investing in employees who might leave the company soon thereafter.

Employee flight is certainly a reasonable fear, but it is one compounded by an environment in which every employer wants trained workers and no one wants to pay for their training. If companies know that their competitors are also trying to hire experienced workers who can "hit the ground running," they don't want to pay to train someone who will soon work for another company. Of course, this across-the-board intransigence virtually guarantees that it will be increasingly hard for any company to find qualified applicants, which will make long-term vacancies more and more common.

John Moredock, an Atlanta-based architect, reports that architecture firms have adopted new computer software to produce architectural drawings and that "almost without exception, vacancies for architects— the few that are advertised—stipulate proficiency in the new software over all else. Firms apparently can't afford to professionally train the people they have, nor are they willing to train new hires [for fear they will be hired away]. It's a macro labor stalemate.... There is no training anymore; businesses just hope to hire it in!"

▲

The Enemy of the Good

One very quick fix could enormously expand the number of qualified candidates: back off the strict requirement that applicants need to have previously done precisely the tasks needed for the vacant job. Instead, see if they could do the job with some training or ramp-up time. Training is an important issue, but with respect to employer complaints about skill gaps, a more immediate concern is employers' unwillingness or inability to allow applicants with the basic skills time to learn the unique aspects of a particular employer and to begin contributing. Hiring on the fundamental character issues and self-management ability, the skills employers repeatedly cite as critical, has its advantages.

One job seeker reports applying for a managing editor position at a small trade magazine. He had writing experience but very little of the skills specific to publishing, such as doing layouts, running production, and coordinating with sales reps. During the interview, the publisher questioned the applicant briefly about his previous work before shoving a bunch of back issues toward him and asking how he would run the magazine. The applicant said he would take the issues home and study them. The publisher then asked when, if hired, the applicant could start. It was Tuesday. "Thursday," the applicant said. "I like that!" said the publisher. "See you on Thursday."

Instead of waiting for the perfect candidate to appear, he took chances on young, smart, motivated—albeit inexperienced—applicants by hiring them on a 90-day probationary period. They would either sink or swim. The employer knew full well that any very talented workers were just cutting their teeth at his company and would leave in a few years, but he could also pay lower salaries and zero training costs because they learned on the job.

Most of the editors he hired were quickly contributing and working hard to build up their résumés.

Letting new hires get up to speed may not work everywhere, but often the constraints lie within management itself. One manager who wished to remain anonymous told me, "My department is too disorganized and undisciplined to have a good program to quickly ramp up new employees for our needs. Thus, we keep looking and looking, and three months go by and we may hire someone at that point, but by then a guy we saw three months ago that had potential and a good work ethic would be starting to contribute."

In fact, companies that exercise this kind of flexibility find that virtually every vacancy is filled immediately. Rich Sheridan, CEO at the software company Menlo Innovations, says his company hires for attitude and invests continually in its employees to get their skill levels up to speed. It works. Sheridan claims, "We never have trouble finding the talent we need!" Unfortunately, the Menlo hiring model appears to be the exception.

Let's do the math on a hypothetical employee vacancy: Assume we have a managerial position that pays $90,000, including an average level of employee benefits that brings the total employment cost up to about $120,000. How much does it cost to leave that job vacant? In sales jobs, where contributions are easy to calculate, it is not uncommon that the figure would be five times compensation costs or more. If the job does not contribute more than the costs of employment, it's hard to understand why it exists, especially in the current cost-cutting context. So it's costing more to keep the vacancy open than to fill it. It's certainly worth searching to avoid a bad hire, but let's not kid ourselves that keeping the position vacant is free. When we are losing money keeping a vacancy unfilled, we can pay for quite a bit of training or ramp-up time and still make money. If your organization does not calculate the cost of keeping vacancies open, how can you possibly know what makes economic sense to do?[31]

The Real Skills Failure

Everyone emerges a loser from this situation. Companies are stuck with often costly vacancies, while job seekers remain unemployed. What makes the situation still worse is that employees are overwhelmingly *willing* to learn the necessary skills to be employed. The Business Roundtable's related survey of employees found 81 percent were willing to get training even outside the workplace, presumably on their own time. However, like employers, 41 percent reported that they were uncertain as to the payoff. Why? Because they did not know what skills would be relevant in their future.[32]

The training gap is further compounded by the fact that the United States has never had a well-developed vocational education program compared to other countries. A half century ago, high school vocational programs were often closely aligned with organized labor: students learned a skill in the classroom, qualified for their union

Figure 5.1
Work-Based Skills Taught in School

Vocational education and training as a share of the upper secondary sector, 2006

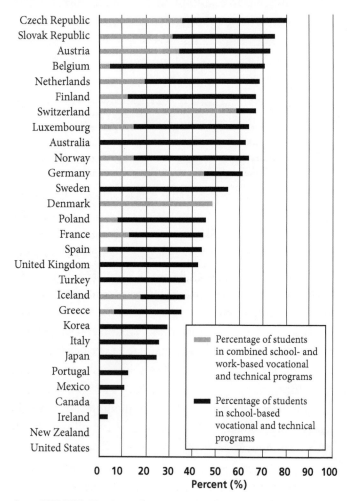

Source: OECD (2008), Education at a Glance 2008: OECD Indicators, *Table C1.1, OECD, Paris.*

card, and went to work in a union shop. Those days are mostly long gone, along with much of the union movement. Employers don't want unions to come back, but that leaves the employer with the responsibility for workplace skills.

Instead, vocational education has become largely a post-high school experience, more so than in most other countries, with the cost burden shared by the students themselves. Enrollments in these programs have ballooned in recent years—powerful evidence that employees are more than willing to accumulate the skills necessary for employment—but funding for such programs has been steadily shrinking,[33] leaving even the most motivated job seekers with fewer options to gain technical skills at the same time that companies are insisting that this is exactly what they must do to be employable. This description also gives us the answer to the puzzle in Table 2.1 in chapter 2 as to why countries like Germany, Switzerland, and the Scandinavian nations report fewer skill gap complaints than the United States despite having much tighter labor markets. They have robust apprenticeship programs and other arrangements that teach work-based skills to students.

Since companies are unlikely to return to the days of lifetime employment, when they could be sure that their training investment wouldn't walk out the door, the only way to address this paradoxical dilemma—in which both supply and demand want the same thing but neither can get it—is to rethink the financing of employer training so that it can pay off in this new environment. That's the subject of the next and final chapter.

CHAPTER 6

The Way Forward

So, to return to the fundamental question this book poses, why can't good people—able, competent women and men—find good jobs when vacancies clearly exist that need to be filled? Surely, part of the problem is that employers are indeed "searching for unicorns": "perfect" fits for what are often imperfectly described and listed jobs.

If not outright broken, the hiring process as commonly practiced is at least part of the problem. It serves short-term budgetary needs far more successfully than it enhances a business's human capital. The temp who can't be hired because, even though she's already doing a very competent job, she doesn't fit the job description? The software program that deep-sixes an applicant not because he lacks experience or credentials, but because the software doesn't recognize his experience and credentials as valid? In another context, this would be the stuff of theater of the absurd.

What can be done about this? The solution we hear about the most is to push the problem off on to the education system. Let them offer more courses tailored to the needs of employers and have them do a better job teaching them. If nothing else changes, we will see even more students jamming the gates of community colleges and more parents and students shelling out money for even more vocationally oriented four-year college programs. Classroom programs are a poor way to teach experience-based skills, though, and the disconnect of students and colleges trying to guess what employers will want remains. The better solution begins by abandoning the conventional wisdom and seeing the problem as it actually is. The heart of the problem is a shortfall in the kinds of skills that are best learned on the job. That has come about because of changes in the way business operates, specifically relying more on outside hiring and less on training and internal development. To crack that nut, we need to figure out how to address the cost issue: How can we make training and skill development pay off for employers?

A Not-So-Novel Idea:
Developing Skills on and for the Job

Happily, this is also the most soluble part of the puzzle. How do you do it? In multiple ways:

In-house training programs

Starting a traditional training program makes sense for many employers because it beats the alternative of keeping vacancies open until the perfect candidate comes along or raising wages enough to attract what is needed. Mechanical Devices, the company earlier described that could not fill its machinist positions, finally set up a 10-week training program to create its own machinists. Out of the first group of 24 trainees, 16 made it to graduation, and the program appears to be a big success for the company.

Employer/employee-shared training programs

The Con-way freight company in Salt Lake City couldn't get enough drivers to meet its demand. While there are plenty of schools that teach truck driving and help applicants get the appropriate licenses, they are expensive enough to keep the supply down. In response, Con-way created driving schools at its truck yards, offering jobs to anyone who completes the training. Those trainee-applicants do not pay up front for the training, but they take the courses on their own time. The employer and the trainees therefore share the costs of training. Bob Petrancosta, a vice president at Con-way, said, "Over an 18-month period since the effort got started, we have graduated nearly 440 drivers and we have a retention rate of 98 percent." The company calculates that the cost of providing the schools was offset by its being able to fill vacancies quickly with candidates it could trust.[34]

The temp and staffing industry has been a leader in using this approach both to give skills to new entrants and to experienced workers. Classes and training are made available for individuals to take on their own time. The temp companies also try to use assignments to build the skills of the temps. The reason in both cases is because they can see the financial payoff by being able to charge more for their temps.

Public-sector/private-sector shared undertakings

In practice, asking government to pay for training probably means state and local entities, not the Feds, and even then you're dealing with severely crunched budgets. But places such as North Carolina have proven this approach can work. The Tarheel State has been using its community college and tech center training programs to lure new employers, offering to select and prepare a workforce for manufacturing operations willing to relocate there. To hold down costs and make sure the training is tailored to specific needs, the programs often use an employer's own systems and equipment.

Broader-based alliances

Taxpayers are sometimes (and understandably) uneasy about giving too much away to lure industries within their borders. What if the transplant takes the training, then jumps to the next state, with the next "great" offer? That's not unheard of.[35] But it certainly makes sense for employers to leverage existing training programs provided by states, employer associations, and other groups. Requiring that job seekers complete community college courses or other programs before they apply for a job, for example, reduces the need to pay for at least the classroom component of training, while also building precision into the external training program. American Electric Power has alliances with 35 technical schools to prepare students for very specific jobs, such as power transmission line mechanic and power generation dispatcher.[36]

Apprenticeship programs

The drawback to many partnering arrangements is that they don't address an employer's need for those work-based skills that can be learned only on the job. Nor do they deal with the fact that both applicants and community colleges are strapped for cash. Traditional apprenticeship programs take care of both problems.

Trainees learn as they work, and they are paid less than the value of the work they contribute. Why does this pay off for the apprentices? Because they know that at the end of the process, they will have very valuable skills and experience, for which they do not have to pay up front. Professional service firms in fields such as law and accounting have long used this approach, as has the medical profession in training doctors. Formal education gets would-be employees only so far in those fields, and to obtain the experience necessary to become proficient requires lots of practice, typically under the supervision of a veteran professional. Meanwhile, the firms get to bill for the apprentices' time at more than the wages they pay them—true of interns and residents in hospitals as well—so they actually make money from them. That's a win all around.

Hazelett Strip-Casting Corporation, a manufacturer of casting equipment, is one of many companies that helped meet their demand for machinists by starting their own apprenticeship programs, in this case in conjunction with a local technical school. The school provides the classroom-based basics, but the company offers paid work experience in a real workplace. Peter Rowan, Hazelett's human resources manager, told me, "After we developed the curriculum and identified the teaching resources, we were able to promote the concept to other local businesses with a similar need for machinists. If you make it easy," he notes, "they will follow."

Do we have evidence that the internal development approach pays off? My colleague Matthew Bidwell addressed this question in a novel but straightforward way by comparing managers hired from the outside to those promoted from within for the same job in large corporations. It took three years for the outsiders to catch up to the performance level of the insiders while it took seven years for those insiders to catch up to the higher pay of the outsiders.[37]

Flying Blind

Modern US companies are extraordinarily sophisticated about virtually all aspects of their supply chains—except when it comes to labor. For some reason they have great difficulty seeing the supply of talent to their organization as the kind of business problem they routinely address in sophisticated, analytical ways. They regularly calculate whether it makes more sense to build or buy components, for example, but seem completely stymied by the idea that training a workforce could be an option. When dealing with suppliers, they have a keen idea of when it makes sense to stop shopping, compromise on their expectations, and cut a deal. Yet most have no idea what it costs them to keep job vacancies open or how to think through when it is best to back off on their requirements and fill a job.

Not coincidentally, the United States has the weakest human resources departments in the industrialized world. The sophisticated planning functions that operated in the HR departments of large corporations a generation ago are long gone, in part because the major workplace irritant to most employers, unions, have effectively disappeared from the private sector, along with those parts of HR associated with combating organized labor. A second, more important reason is that the long period of very slack labor markets that began with the arrival of the baby boomers in the early 1970s (interrupted only by the short period from roughly 1998 to 2001) made the HR function relatively simple. In particular, recruiting on a just-in-time basis was easy. Students competed to get more business-oriented academic training, and the nearly constant restructuring of companies that led to layoffs also made it easy to hire experienced talent that had been trained in big companies. As HR problems diminished, the human resource function was cut back more and more.

The relative ease of recruiting talent contributed to a new approach to business competitiveness, which was to redirect business strategy quickly by hiring in new, experienced talent that could reshuffle a business's competencies. That demand for outside talent contributed to the decline in the training and internal development of candidates: Why "make" when it is so easy to "buy"? A single company or even several companies can pursue that approach, but when they all try to hire the skills they need from their competitors, we have a problem.

The weakness of the HR function has made it difficult to identify what is in an employer's best interest when confronted with these problems. Only theorists believe that individual businesses always do what is in their best interest. Those who are close to the action recognize that businesses are run by real people, who are fallible and who are increasingly pushed to do more and more with less and less. The kind of sophisticated analyses that would show whether it makes more sense to train than keep trying to hire, whether it saves money to bring on less-than-perfect applicants and let them get up to speed, and whether the current hiring process that takes humans out of the system causes more problems than it solves, are now beyond the capabilities of all but the very largest HR organizations.

If you are an executive reading this and doubt this argument, I urge you to go directly to your HR department and ask for evidence as to whether the last layoffs saved more money than they cost or what it costs the organization to leave a position vacant and whether they are being left open too long. See if you can get an answer.

Money Talks

One final reason the skills gap argument has gotten so much traction, and the actual causes of the supply-demand job mismatch are so poorly understood: the associations and organizations that serve employers dominate the discussion. Such entities have the resources to get arguments in front of the public, but they do not have the time or perhaps the inclination to examine those arguments carefully. They are also reluctant to tell employers that they should do something the employers don't necessarily want to do, such as provide more training. The Business Roundtable being a notable exception.

The glaring example of the gap between reality and easy arguments is the blame placed on schools for the presumed skills gap problem: employers have been saying for decades that their big problems with those entering the workforce are workplace attitudes, *not* academic skills, and what they want now is experienced workers, not recent grads, so how did the argument get "spun" to blame schools?

The United States is at the moment the only country in the world where the notion that employers are simply the consumers of skills is seriously considered. That may help explain why we are also the world leader in the creation of a for-profit training industry that meets the skill demand, where individuals pay close to the full cost of getting the skills they need. Indeed, for-profits now provide *50 percent* of all skills credentials. One could make the argument that individuals should be the ones to pay because they are the ones who will get the benefits, but we also know that only those who have the finances will be able to pay, and even then, the supply of trained applicants might not be enough to meet employer needs. Also, if individuals have to pay for the skills they need, they aren't going to do so unless there is a payoff in the form of better wages. So one way or another, employers are going to have to pay.

Teaching work-based skills outside the workplace is both inefficient and impractical in the long run. What's more, it makes no sense for the employers, as consumers of skills, to remain an arm's-length distance from the schools that produce those skills. There are better ways for employers to handle these issues even from the perspective of their self-interest.

Where should we be heading instead? We are not going to get a national system of training. Nor are we going to get European-style apprenticeship programs, which require employers to make long-term commitments. The country is too big and too fragmented to make any arrangements like those work. But there is a proven middle ground.

In the mid-1990s the topic of building a better transition from school to work was hot, in part because employers were getting concerned about a skills deficit. (The momentum died, however, with the 2001 recession and a new administration in Washington.) The main lesson from those policy discussions was that getting employers and schools closer together in the form of co-op programs, internships, and collaborations that integrate classroom and work experience does wonders for everyone. Students learn academic material more easily when they see practical uses for it; employees and students alike benefit from having contact with one another (the employees take their roles more seriously, and the students learn more about what the workplace requires); and in the end, employers see graduates who are better prepared for jobs.

The constraint on building these arrangements has always been on the employer side: how to get them to engage in these efforts when the payoff to them is not immediate. The present, debilitating disconnect between job supply and job demand suggests that the time has finally come for employers to develop a more realistic sense of what their own interests are with respect to workforce issues and what best serves both their interests and the well-being of society as a whole.

Notes

1 Bill Roberts, "Can They Keep Our Lights On?" *HR Magazine* 55, no. 6 (June 2010): 62–68.

2 Motoko Rich, "Factory Jobs Return, but Employers Find Skills Shortage," *New York Times*, July 1, 2010, online edition.

3 For a review of these claims, see Ben Braden, "Are Employers to Blame for the Skills Gap?" *US News and World Report*, November 18, 2011. See money.usnews.com/money/careers/articles/2011/11/18/are-employers-to-blame-for-the-skills-gap. Accessed January 18, 2012.

4 For a review of prior studies and some contemporary evidence, see Vera Brenčič, "Do Employers Respond to the Costs of Continued Search?" *Oxford Bulletin of Economics & Statistics* 72, no. 2 (April 2010): 221–45. See web.ebscohost.com/ehost/detail?sid=92d5a89b-0fae-47d5-91f3-eb59 39eab165%40sessionmgr4&vid=1&hid=9&bdata=JnNpdGU9ZWhvc3Q tbGl2ZQ%3d%3d#db=keh&AN=48159806. Accessed January 18, 2012.

5 It is certainly possible to have job requirements that are so specific that there is no market for them. But if that is the case, we would expect the employer to be growing the requirements from within: Who else would have any interest in producing them?

6 For a review of assertions that something is different about the labor market in this recession and a debunking of those assertions, see Jesse Rothstein, "The Labor Market Four Years into the Crisis: Assessing Structural Explanations," Cambridge, MA: The National Bureau of Economic Research Working Paper #17966, 2012. For specific evidence that the rate at which vacancies are being filled now is similar to the past, see, e.g., Murat Tasci and John Linder, "Has the Beveridge Curve Shifted?" *Economic Trends*, Federal Reserve Bank of Cleveland, 2010. See www.clevelandfed.org/research/trends/2010/0810/02labmar.cfm.

7 That's according to Steve B. Vaisey, "Education and Its Discontents, 1972–2002: Overqualification in America," *Social Forces* 85, no. 2 (December 2006).

8 See, e.g., James J. Heckman and Paul A. LaFontaine, "Bias-Corrected Estimates of GED Returns," *Journal of Labor Economics*, July 2006, Vol. 24 Issue 3, pp. 661-700. Some employers have in the past been reluctant to hire candidates who are far overqualified for their jobs for fear that those candidates will be unhappy in the jobs and eventually quit. Given that so few jobs last a long time now, that concern seems to have dissipated. It is certainly true that if we had perfectly efficient labor markets, we would not see such a situation. But we don't have them.

9 *The New York Times* has written a number of stories documenting such unpaid internships. See, for example, www.nytimes.com/roomfordebate/2012/02/04/do-unpaid-internships-exploit-college-students. Accessed January 18, 2012.

10 The extent to which employers are not accepting applicants from the unemployed is great enough that the Equal Opportunities Employment Commission is investigating whether such behavior amounts to illegal discrimination. See http://www.eeoc.gov/eeoc/newsroom/release/2-14-11a.cfm. Accessed January 18, 2012.

11 For evidence on the skills of older workers and of discrimination against them, see Peter Cappelli and Bill Novelli, *Managing the Older Workforce: How to Prepare for the New Organizational Order*, Boston: Harvard Business Review Press, 2011.

12 These two examples can be found at Mark Whitehouse, "Some Firms Struggle to Hire Despite High Unemployment," August 9, 2010, *Wall Street Journal*. See online.wsj.com/article/SB1000142405274870489 5004575395491314812452.html. See the Bureau of Labor Statistics for statistics data for machinist wages: www.bls.gov/oes/current/oes514041.htm. Accessed January 18, 2012.

13 Treva Lind, "Mine Labor in Demand; Wages Soar," *Journal of Business* 27, no. 21 (January 5, 2012): A1–A12.

14 For the 2011 results, see ManpowerGroup Migration for Work Survey, August 2011. See candidate.manpower.com/wps/wcm/connect/58 576e0047e907f3a23fe31dc7731a4f/RelocationSurveyResults_0811. pdf?MOD=AJPERES. Accessed January 18, 2012. For the 1990s experience, see Peter Cappelli, *The New Deal at Work: Managing the Market-Driven Workforce*, Boston: Harvard Business School Press, 1999, chap. 3.

15 For a survey of these studies, see Peter Cappelli, "Rethinking the 'Skills Gap,'" *California Management Review* 37, no. 4 (Summer 1995): 108–24.

16 Research Report—Career Advisory Board Job Preparedness Indicator, 2011, Career Advisory Board, presented by DeVry University and Harris Interactive Interviewing. See careeradvisoryboard.com/public/ uploads/2011/11/Job-Preparedness-Indicator-Research-Report.pdf. Accessed January 18, 2012.

17 For a review of the evidence, especially in the United Kingdom, see Alison Wolf, Liam Aspin, Edmund Waite, and Katerina Ananiadoum, "The Rise and Fall of Workplace Basic Skills Programmes: Lessons for Policy and Practice," *Oxford Review of Education* 36, no. 4 (2010): 385–405. The United Kingdom had a very similar policy debate in which the assertion was that poor levels of basic academic skills among workers were hurting the economy. Closer inspection found that employers did not in fact see this problem, and efforts to raise those skills had little effect on performance.

18 See nces.ed.gov/fastfacts/index.asp?faq=FFOption1#faqFFOption1. Accessed January 18, 2012.

19 "Trends in High School Dropout and Completion Rates in the United States: 1972–2009." See nces.ed.gov/pubs2012/2012006.pdf. Accessed January 18, 2012.

20 The OECD's comparative educational outcomes are known
as the Programme for International Student Assessment
studies and can be seen at www.oecd.org/document/53/0,3746
,en_32252351_46584327_46584821_1_1_1_1,00.html. Accessed
January 18, 2012.

21 Anthony Carnavale and his colleagues at the Georgetown Center on
Education and the Workforce assert that the nation faces a serious
shortfall of college graduates. See www9.georgetown.edu/grad/gppi/
hpi/cew/pdfs/ExecutiveSummary-web.pdf. Accessed January 18, 2012.
Paul Harrington and Andrew Sum at Northeastern University's Center
for Labor Market Studies counter that such assertions assume that
there is no overeducation in jobs now. They point out, for example,
that such an assumption means that the 57 percent of bartenders
who have had at least some college education need that education
to be bartenders. Carnavale counters that the rising wage premium
for workers with college degrees must indicate that such education
is valued. That assertion is wrong. The wage premium for college
is measured as the gap between wages for workers without college
degrees and those with college degrees. The wage premium has grown
because wages for those without college degrees have collapsed. The
increase in real wages for those with college degrees has been trivial.
If the question is whether you as an individual are better off with
a college degree, Carnavale and colleagues are surely right. If the
question is whether the economy needs more college graduates, at
least by these criteria, Harrington and Sum are right. For the exchange
between them, see *The New England Journal of Higher Education*,
March 18, 2012.

22 For evidence on college majors, see bachelor's degrees conferred by
degree-granting institutions, by field of study: Selected years, 1970–71
through 2008–09, *Digest of Educational Statistics*, NCES, Table 282.
See nces.ed.gov/programs/digest/d10/tables/dt10_282.asp?referrer=list.
Accessed January 18, 2012.

23 See Richard B. Freeman and Daniel L. Goroff, *Science and Engineering
Careers in the United States: An Analysis of Markets and Employment*,
Chicago: University of Chicago Press, 2009, Introduction, p. 1.

24 See Peter Cappelli, "Why Is It So Hard to Find IT Workers?" *Organizational Dynamics* 2 (2001): 87–99.

25 Aysegul Sahin, Joseph Song, Giorgio Topa, and Giovanni L. Violante, "Measuring Mismatch in the US Labor Market," New York: Federal Reserve Bank of New York working paper, 2001.

26 Christopher S. Rugaber, "Employer Demands Mean Some Jobs Go Unfilled: Required Skill Set Expands So Many Are Left Unqualified in Own Field," Associated Press, November 10, 2010. See www.msnbc.msn.com/id/39604781/ns/business-careers/t/employer-demands-mean-some-jobs-go-unfilled/#.T1uM5YES01I. Accessed January 18, 2012.

27 See post.nyssa.org/nyssa-news/2010/03/beat-the-resumescreen-algorithm.html, http://ezinearticles.com/?What-You-Dont-Know-About-Resume-Screening-Software-Could-Be-Sabotaging-Your-Job-Search&id=2781294, http://www.theladders.com/career-advice/resume-technology-resume-format-machine-friendly. Accessed January 18, 2012.

28 For a review of data on the extent of training, see Lisa M. Lynch and Sandra E. Black, "Beyond the Incidence of Employer-Provided Training," *Industrial and Labor Relations Review* 52, no. 1 (1998): 64–81, and Harley Frazis, Maury Gittleman, and Mary Joyce. "Correlates of Training: An Analysis Using Both Employer and Employee Characteristics," *Industrial and Labor Relations Review* 53, no. 3 (2000): 443–62.

29 Mike Collins, "America's Skilled Worker Shortage—Part II," *Industrial Maintenance and Plant Operation* 72, no. 2 (March 2011): 62.

30 Mike Collins, "America's Skilled Worker Shortage," *Industrial Maintenance and Plant Operation*, 72, no. 1 (January 2011): 44.

31 Calculators for assessing the costs of standing vacancies are readily available, and they may require either data that are hard to get or assumptions that are not completely accurate. But it is important to remember that the calculations do not have to be perfect to be useful. Without them, we are flying blind. Some calculators include the following: www.hcamag.com/resources/Recruitment/calculating-the-cost-of-vacancies/113915/; www.volt.com/uploadedFiles/voltcom/ Volt_Workforce_Solutions/Resources/TopicBrief_COV.pdf; www. employersoverload.com/employers/resources-clients/the-high-cost-of-job-vacancies; www.lasocareers.com/clients/vacant-position-costs. html. Accessed January 18, 2012.

32 Fifty-five percent of the employees were confident that they knew what skills would be relevant for their careers. Given what we know about overconfidence biases being especially great about issues we know little about, that confidence is quite likely inflated, and it also begs the question as to how far out they were projecting.

33 For a quick guide to these trends, see "The Burden of Budget Cuts," *New York Times* online edition, March 1, 2012. See www.nytimes. com/interactive/2012/03/02/business/the-burden-of-budget-cuts. html?ref=dealbook. Accessed January 18, 2012.

34 For more details on this story, see Chris Arnold, "A Labor Mismatch Means Trucking Jobs Go Unfilled," October 13, 2011, National Public Radio. See www.con-way.com/en/about_con_way/newsroom/press_ releases/Dec_2010/2010_dec_07/. Accessed January 18, 2012.

35 For examples of the debate, see Motoko Rich, "Private Sector Gets Job Skills; Public Gets Bill," *New York Times* online edition, January 7, 2012. Accessed January 18, 2012.

36 See AEP Technical School Alliances, www.aep.com/careers/ collegerelations/techschool.aspx. Accessed January 18, 2012.

37 Matthew Bidwell, "Paying More to Get Less: The Effects of External Hiring versus Internal Mobility," *Administrative Science Quarterly* 56 (2011): 369-407.

Index

About the Author

Peter Cappelli is the George W. Taylor professor of management at The Wharton School and director of Wharton's Center for Human Resources. He codirected the US Department of Education's National Center on the Educational Quality of the Workforce in the mid-1990s and served on several National Academy of Sciences reports on workforce issues. He is also a research associate at the National Bureau of Economic Research in Cambridge, Massachusetts, served as senior adviser to the Kingdom of Bahrain for employment policy from 2003 to 2005, and since 2007, is a distinguished scholar of the Ministry of Manpower for Singapore.

Cappelli's recent research examines changes in employment relations in the United States and their implications. He writes a monthly column on workforce issues for Human Resource Executive Online and has contributed to the *Wall Street Journal,* the *Washington Post, Bloomberg Businessweek,* and other news venues. His books include *Managing the Older Worker: How to Prepare for the New Organizational Order* (with Bill Novelli), *The India Way: How India's Business Leaders Are Revolutionizing Management* (with Harbir Singh, Jitendra Singh, and Michael Useem), *Talent on Demand: Managing Talent in the Age of Uncertainty, and The New Deal at Work: Managing the Market-Driven Workforce.*

He was named by *HR Magazine* as one of 2011's top 20 most influential thinkers and by Vault.com as one the 25 most important people working in the area of human capital. In 2006, he was elected a fellow of the National Academy of Human Resources. He received the 2009 PRO award from the International Association of Corporate and Professional Recruiters for contributions to human resources.

Cappelli has degrees in industrial relations from Cornell University and a doctorate in labor economics from the University of Oxford, where he was a Fulbright scholar.

About Wharton Digital Press

Wharton Digital Press was established to inspire bold, insightful thinking within the global business community. In the tradition of The Wharton School of the University of Pennsylvania and its online business journal *Knowledge@ Wharton*, Wharton Digital Press uses innovative digital technologies to help managers meet the challenges of today and tomorrow.

As an entrepreneurial publisher, Wharton Digital Press delivers relevant, accessible, conceptually sound, and empirically based business knowledge to readers wherever and whenever they need it. Its format ranges from ebooks and enhanced ebooks to mobile apps and print books available through print-on-demand technology. Directed to a general business audience, the Press's areas of interest include management and strategy, innovation and entrepreneurship, finance and investment, leadership, marketing, operations, human resources, social responsibility, business-government relations, and more.

wdp.wharton.upenn.edu

UNIVERSITY of PENNSYLVANIA

About The Wharton School

The Wharton School of the University of Pennsylvania—founded in 1881 as the first collegiate business school—is recognized globally for intellectual leadership and ongoing innovation across every major discipline of business education. The most comprehensive source of business knowledge in the world, Wharton bridges research and practice through its broad engagement with the global business community. The School has more than 4,800 undergraduate, MBA, executive MBA, and doctoral students; more than 9,000 annual participants in executive education programs; and an alumni network of 86,000 graduates.

www.wharton.upenn.edu

Made in the USA
Lexington, KY
05 October 2012